BLACK BEAUTY
ANNUAL

£1.00

FIVE FOR SILVER

One bright morning as Jenny knelt picking bluebells in the woods near York Cottage she heard the sound of horse's hoofs drawing nearer. Instinctively she looked across the copse where she had left Black Beauty, but he was still there, contentedly munching the rich green grass.

Suddenly through a clearing Jenny saw a pretty dark-haired girl approaching, riding a handsome white horse. When the girl saw Jenny she reined in her horse sharply, and a look of relief spread across her worried face.

"Oh, Miss Jenny, I am glad to see you!" she cried. "Is your Father at home? My Grandfather needs his help badly."

"No, he is still out on his rounds," replied Jenny. "Beauty cast a shoe this morning and I have just been to the blacksmith's for a new one. Father borrowed a chestnut mare from the Squire to visit his patients this morning. He was rather surprised that Squire Armstrong offered help in this way . . . you know what he is like!" she ended with a rueful smile.

"I do indeed!" cried Carla angrily. "He is a hard, unfeeling man with a heart of stone. Have you heard that he plans to turn Grandfather and me out of our cottage? The Squire says that now that Grandfather can no longer tend the sheep on his estate, he will have to find a new shepherd, and we must find a new home!"

"But Adam Greenshaw has lived in that cottage for years!" protested Jenny. "I remember old Granny Jameson telling me how she remembered your Grandfather bringing his bride home there. And it has been your home, Carla, ever since your parents died. Surely the Squire has another empty cottage on that vast estate for a new shepherd?"

"There *are* other cottages, it is true," agreed Carla. "But if we stay, the Squire says we must pay rent, and where is the money to come from? My Grandfather could never save a penny for times like this, and I do not wish to go into service and let him be forced into the charity poorhouse. That is why I was coming to see your father to ask him to help."

"Oh, I'm sure he will do all he can," Jenny assured her quickly. "I will leave a message for him to go and see your Grandfather as soon as he returns. Meanwhile, the boys and I will go with you to your cottage in case you need help before Father arrives."

As Jenny mounted Black Beauty, a flutter of wings above her head caused her to look up and smile. "Magpies," she cried to Carla. "One, two, three, four, five . . . five for silver, so the old rhyme says."

"Well, we could certainly do with a little silver now," replied Carla, as she watched the magpies fly away over the trees. "Then we could pay the Squire's rent and stay in our home."

"The boys are over at Cooper's Farm helping with the haymaking," said Amy, when the two girls arrived at York Cottage. "I've just heard the news, Carla. 'Tis a Christian shame so it is . . . the Squire should be ashamed of himself, turning a man out of his home after a lifetime's honest toil."

"We'd better be getting to your cottage," interrupted Jenny hastily, seeing that Carla was almost on the point of tears. I'll just take a lump of sugar for Beauty!"

"That horse eats more sugar than the entire family put together!" retorted Amy rather tartily; but she pretended not to see the *two* lumps which Jenny pocketed for Beauty.

The two girls galloped quickly over to the old shepherd's cottage where, to their great surprise, they found Kevin and Ned already there, along with Farmer Cooper who was remonstrating loudly with two men who were putting old Adam's furniture outside in the road in front of his cottage.

"We've 'ad our orders that this cottage 'as ter be emptied by termorrer!" one man said, but he looked very ashamed as he spoke. "I'm right sorry, but I 'ave ter carry my orders out or I'll lose my job!"

The farmer and the children looked on helplessly as the men walked towards the door to continue their task. But Beauty had other ideas and suddenly he reared up against the porch, refusing to let them in.

"Good for you, Beauty!" called Ned, but although frightened the removal men began to get very angry and threatened to whip Beauty.

"Don't you dare!" cried Jenny, "or it will be the worse for you."

"Indeed it will," added a familiar voice, and up rode Doctor Gordon on the Squire's chestnut mare. "I've just had a word with Armstrong," he went on firmly, "and he has finally agreed to let Adam and Carla stay on a few days until they find somewhere else to live. After all, he does not want to be held responsible for bringing on a bad attack of Adam's bronchitis with perhaps very serious consequences. Now come along, men, get all this furniture back again. You too, boys, lend them a hand before it starts to rain!"

Grumbling a little beneath their breath, the

men did as the Doctor asked, and Jenny and Carla went indoors to arrange it.

"Goodness, it *is* cold in here," said Jenny, shivering a little. "Let's light a fire."

"It keeps smoking," said Carla. "I think there must be an old bird's nest up there, blocking the air."

"Well, let's see," said Doctor Gordon, taking up a long-handled brush and poking it hard up the chimney.

A mass of soot fell down and a mess of blackened leaves and feathers. "I think that's what's been causing the trouble," he said. "Oh, wait a moment . . . I can feel something else."

Suddenly, as the Doctor gave an extra hard poke, down fell a soot-covered object, followed by three or four more, and lay there in the hearth for everyone to see.

"Whatever are they?" asked Jenny, picking one up rather gingerly and showing it to her Father.

"Why, I believe they are made of silver!"

cried James Gordon. "Yes, here is a hallmark on the statue. Try and clean the others up, girls, and then we must try and find out who they belong to."

"I can tell you that," said a voice as old Adam Greenshaw hobbled into his cottage. "I've just heard how you've had a word on my behalf with the Squire. Thank 'ee kindly, Doctor."

"It was nothing, old chap," said the Doctor gruffly, for as usual he hated to be thanked for any kindness to others. "Now tell me about this silver."

"Well, Doctor Gordon, I reckon it is the silver which was stolen nigh over a hundred year ago from Eddington Hall when the present lord's grandfather was alive," said Adam. "They caught the thieves near here, but never recovered the silver. This cottage was empty at the time . . . the thieves must have hidden the silver in the chimney.

"You may well be right, Adam," said the Doctor. "Now if you will trust me with this

silver, I will take it to the Squire and Lord Eddington and tell them the whole story."

"Take it, Doctor, and do as you wish," urged Adam eagerly. "I am only glad it has been found."

So the Doctor collected up all the silver from Jenny, Ned and Kevin, who had been admiring it, and set off to the Hall.

The Gordons and Carla eagerly awaited his return, but Adam calmly set about mending a broken fence near the cottage, seemingly unperturbed by all the excitement.

But even *he* rose to meet the Squire as he rode up on his horse, realising that it must be good news from the unaccustomed good-humour on Armstrong's face.

"Lord Eddington was so pleased to get his silver back that he has purchased your cottage from me and he has agreed to keep it in good repair for you and your granddaughter for the rest of your lives," he explained genially. "And Lord Eddington says also that since most of your life was spent in his service on the estate, he will pay you a pension large enough for your needs."

"Oh, Squire, that *is* wonderful news!" cried Jenny, as Black Beauty also whinnied his approval. Then, turning to Carla, she added with a chuckle, "You see, those five magpies certainly did mean silver!"

"Indeed they did, Jenny," agreed Carla happily. "Now, thanks to them and to your Father, Lord Eddington has got back his family silver and we still have a roof over our head. Those magpies certainly brought us luck."

And she waved goodbye to Jenny and the boys as they went home to tell Amy the good news.

Double Talk

Here are some 'horsey' expressions which have another meaning as well as the more obvious one.

A DONKEY'S BREAKFAST

This is a merchant navy term for a straw-filled mattress.

AN ASS WITH TWO PANNIERS

The laughing expression given to a man who escorts two ladies at the same time, one on each arm.

TO RIDE THE HORSE WITH TEN TOES

This is another way of saying that a person has to walk – he is the horse with the ten toes.

WHOSE MARE IS DEAD?

Another way of asking what is wrong or what is the matter. Shakespeare used the expression in one of his historical plays.

A COLT

Not a young horse in this case, but the barrister who once attended a Serjeant-at-law at his induction. It is also the old name for the whipping rope used on disobedient young sailors in the navy in days gone by.

A STALKING-HORSE

Something or someone used to mislead others, dating back to the days when men hid behind their horses until they were near enough to shoot game.

HORSE FACTS and FANCIES

THE AGE OF A HORSE

Thrice the age of a dog
Is that of a horse,
But thrice the age of a horse
Is that of a man.

BAYARDO'S LEAP

Near Sleaford there are three large stones, each some thirty yards apart. They are known locally as 'Bayardo's Leap'. The stones recall a story about Bayardo, the magnificent horse belonging to the knight Rinaldo. One day as Rinaldo was out riding, a demon sprang up on the horse behind the knight and tried to attack Rinaldo. But Bayardo took three mighty leaps onto three stepping stones, unseating the demon and drowning him in the water.

CENTAURS

Centaurs were mythological beasts with the bodies of horses and the heads of men. They were believed to dwell in Thessaly and to have taught the inhabitants of the island to become expert horsemen.

HORSES AND HAWKS

Although the name mews is given to stables where horses are kept, the word comes from two old French and Latin words meaning a cage used by hawks when they are moulting! The reason for the name being used in a horsey connection is because in the 17th century the royal stables were built on a piece of ground which was formerly the royal Mews where the king's hawks were kept. Today the mews have been converted into flats and make very desirable London residences.

LED BY THE NOSE

Anyone who is willing to be guided by another person of stronger character or beliefs is said to be led by the nose, a phrase recalling the fact that donkeys and horses are led by the nose by bridle and bit. Incidentally, horses are counted by 'noses' and not 'heads', as are cattle.

THE BLACK HORSE OF CHARING CROSS

Today the statue of Charles I can be seen in Whitehall, but at one time it could have been seen at Charing Cross, to the delight once more of his Royalist supporters after the return to England of his son, Charles II. A little sentimental rhyme was composed for the occasion, which is still sung today as a nursery rhyme:

As I was going by Charing Cross,
I saw a black man upon a black horse,
They told me it was King Charles the First –
Oh, dear, my heart was ready to burst!

HARVEST HOME

"Oh, Simeon, I *am* enjoying myself!" cried Jenny as she settled herself more comfortably among the hay in the cart. "I am glad I decided to ride over with the boys' lunch today."

"And we are right glad to see you, Miss Jenny," replied Simeon, his face breaking into a beaming smile, as he gently urged Black Beauty forward down the lane. "When old Dobbin cast a shoe, carrying the hay to the barn would have been nigh impossible without your help. And we want everything finished for tonight's harvest home in the church hall."

"Yes, we are all looking forward to that very much," added Jenny. "Father and Amy are coming too, and I do believe that even the

Squire is condescending to look in for a few minutes."

"Did you hear that, Reuben?" called Simeon, as they drove up over the cobbled farmyard towards where a farm labourer was leaning, arms folded against a haystack.

The man's face darkened with anger and he said contemptuously, "Well, that is one man who won't be welcomed. And if I am on the door, it will be shut in his face."

"Now then, Reuben lad, still thy bitter tongue!" pleaded Simeon. "You know that all must be made welcome at the harvest home. Remember old Lord Eddington only gave each worker a bag of meal and a sack of corn as his own gift when t'harvest were done. Squire

Armstrong was well within his right to refuse to carry on with the old custom. After all, it is his estate harvest, we only work for him."

"Aye, but it would have cost him very little, and it means so much to the men, especially those with families," retorted Reuben bitterly. "The man has no heart."

Jenny privately agreed with all Reuben's remarks, but knowing that her doctor father would disapprove of any adverse comments she might make to the estate workers, she wisely said nothing.

"Miss Jenny," said Reuben suddenly as he and Simeon deftly stowed the hay away in the barn. "Would you lend me Black Beauty for a while before you go home? I need him for a little job I have to do."

Jenny looked doubtful, especially as she saw Reuben eyeing the full bags and sacks lying in the barn. Then, quietening her conscience by thinking that if she did not ask questions she would not *really* know anything, she reluctantly nodded.

"But we must have Beauty back home before tea," she insisted "We need him to take us all to the village later."

"I'll harness him back to the trap myself," promised Reuben. "You go back to the hay fields and rest beneath a shady tree. I'll bring Black Beauty to you there."

True to his word, Reuben arrived back in less than an hour with Beauty in the trap, and Jenny and Ned set off home, while Kevin walked with Albert so that he might see his pet rabbits on the way home.

"Now, don't eat too much tea or there won't be room for all that splendid supper the village ladies are preparing," warned Amy with a twinkle in her eye as she put a plate of buttered scones and jam and cream down on the table. "Doctor Gordon is still away at the Squire's attending that spoilt niece of his. Fancy sending a carriage and pair to collect a doctor . . . some people have more money than sense!"

Just then Kevin rushed in, looking rather alarmed. "Jenny, the Squire's carriage has just driven up and Father and Squire Armstrong are arguing loudly. It appears that the Squire is accusing us of using Black Beauty in some plot to steal his grain. Do you know anything about it?"

"By the look on her face she does," commented Amy drily. "You'd better go out and make your peace, Jenny . . . if you can!"

Jenny got up from the table reluctantly and went slowly outside. The look on the two men's faces as she approached did little to raise her spirits.

"Jenny, will you please bring Beauty here," said her father sternly.

Rather bewildered, but fearing to ask too many questions, Jenny did as she was bid.

Squire Armstrong bent down and carefully examined Beauty's hoofs. "As I thought . . . traces of meal!" he cried triumphantly. "This animal was used by the thieves, probably with your daughter's co-operation!"

"I didn't help, but I did lend them Beauty . . . and perhaps I did know what was planned!" ended Jenny with a sudden burst of honesty. "But I don't blame them in the least. "You *are* mean, Squire Armstrong, and you *deserve* to lose some of your harvest!"

"There, Doctor Gordon, what do you think of your daughter now?" sneered the Squire.

"I think she acted misguidedly, but I have great sympathy with the men," replied the Doctor, with a comforting smile at Jenny. "I don't think you realise what a difference that free grain made to families, Armstrong!"

"Stop trying to whitewash them, Gordon" retorted the Squire. "Those two will lose their jobs for sure and . . ."

He broke off suddenly as old Simeon came running up, panting and breathless. "Young Master James has fallen into the mill stream!" he called. "Reuben's trying to hold him afloat, but the currents very strong and he's beginning to tire."

The Squire's face whitened as he realised what had befallen his small godson, who was spending a few days with him at his home.

But before he could speak, James Gordon had seized a strong piece of rope which was always kept hanging on a nearby fence in case of emergencies and, mounting Beauty, he set off in the direction of the mill.

"Get more help if you can, Armstrong!" he called over his shoulder. "I'll do what I can."

"Go, Beauty, go!" encouraged Jenny as she watched her father riding as hard as he could over fences and ditches. "Pray God that he is in time!"

As if knowing just what was expected of him, Beauty flew swift as the wind and in far less time than usual, the horse and rider arrived at the old mill.

Doctor Gordon took in the situation at a glance. Reuben was still holding the small boy's head above water, but his tired face was showing signs of strain.

Quickly the Doctor made a lasso with his rope

and, taking care, threw it so that it snaked through the air to tighten securely around both Reuben and the boy.

"Pull, Beauty, pull!" urged James Gordon as he guided the horse towards the green grass, the ends of the rope knotted tightly around Beauty's saddle.

Slowly, the two figures were dragged to safety and lay panting on the grass. A quick glance, with an answering nod from Reuben, showed the Doctor that he was alright, so James quickly turned his attention to the boy. Although shocked and trembling, the child only had a few superficial bruises, and James sighed that all was well.

He was just helping Reuben to his feet when the Squire's carriage sped up, carrying several unfamiliar occupants including three burly farm workers and Jenny, with Ned and Kevin clinging to the top with the coachman.

"He's safe!" called Doctor Gordon.

"Thanks to you, Gordon!" cried the Squire in a choked voice. "How can I thank you?"

"By saying no more about the missing grain," replied the good doctor at once. "Remember that all my efforts would have been in vain if Reuben here had not dived in to save the boy in the first place. Surely your godson's life is worth a few sacks of corn?"

For a moment the Squire hesitated, then he smiled. "Nothing more will be said," he answered and then he added as an afterthought, "But I shall expect a fine supper at the harvest home tonight."

As they watched the Squire stride away with his godson in his arms, the others couldn't resist a laugh as they heard the Doctor mutter. "If that man ever gives anything away without expecting something in return I'll eat a plate of Beauty's oats for my supper!"

Horseshoes, Horse Lore and the Horseman's Word

Legends, superstitions, and fanciful beliefs have surrounded the horse since it was first domesticated by man – thousands of years ago. Horse folklore has been handed down through countless generations, and some of it is still believed today.

One of the superstitions which has survived best of all is the belief in the powers of horseshoes as good luck tokens. For centuries now, in every country where horses are shod, the horseshoe has been hung over doors as a protective amulet.

Horseshoes were first thought to be lucky for three main reasons. They are made of iron, signifying strength; they are in the shape of a lunar symbol; and perhaps most important, they are made by blacksmiths, who were once believed to have all sorts of magical powers, including the ability to talk to fairies.

Should you happen to see a horseshoe lying in the road, you should be very pleased at your find, and if the shoe has been cast from the near hind leg of a grey mare, then it really is your lucky day. In some parts of the country the best thing to do would be to pick the horseshoe up, spit on it, make a wish, and throw it over your left shoulder, without looking back.

But the more general custom, of course, is to take it home with you and hang it over a door. Opinions differ about the best way to hang it. Some people would advise you to hang it with the horns pointing downwards, but others would say this is quite wrong, as it allows the good luck to spill out.

If you believe in the superstition that seven years bad luck will follow the breaking of a mirror, don't despair next time you break one. Simply lead a horse through the house and the spell will be broken. And if you have the bad luck to spill salt, just lead a horse – but only a white or grey will do – through the kitchen, and the spell will be broken.

The colour grey is thought to be very lucky in horses, and there was a time when grey horses were often used to draw bridal carriages. If the bride or groom saw a grey horse on the way to the church, they were sure to have a long and happy marriage.

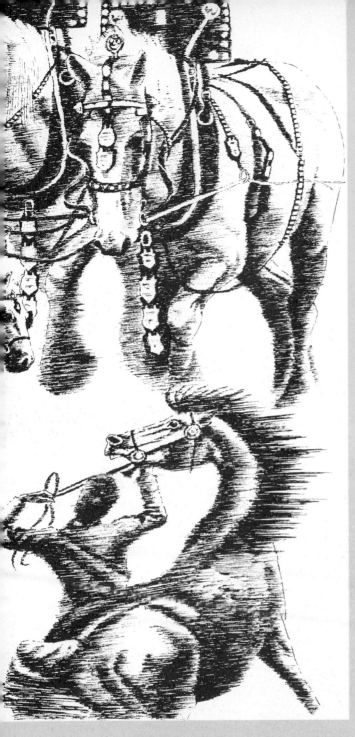

One white foot, buy a horse,
Two white feet, try a horse,
Three white feet, look well about him,
Four white feet, do without him.

When you had bought a new horse it was important to take precautions to safeguard it against danger, particularly as horses were thought to be very susceptible to spells from witches and the evil eye. Many charms and amulets were hung around horses' necks and in their stables, and this idea has partly survived to this day in horse brasses, which were originally intended to ward off the evil eye.

Horse brasses were traditionally cast in shapes which symbolised a long and happy life, such as rayed suns, crescent moons, hearts, wheels, lotus flowers, and one shape which was originally a symbol of purity, but which has since taken on a different and sinister meaning, the swastika.

As well as being susceptible to spells from witches, horses were also believed to be quite unable to resist the powers of a particular charm which could be used on them by humans. This was called the Horseman's Word.

The charm was known to a select few horsemen, grooms, carters, and blacksmiths, and it consisted of whispering just a few secret words. Any horse, however wild and untamable, would then fall completely under the will of the speaker. It was said that the charm could stop a wild stallion in full gallop.

The Horseman's Word was a closely guarded secret, passed to others at clandestine meetings only on a solemn oath of secrecy. In Scotland, those privileged few who knew the secrets joined together in an elite society called the Brotherhood of the Horseman's Word.

It is possible that the famous American horse trainer, John S. Rarey, who tamed many completely unapproachable horses in the mid 19th century, may have used the Horseman's Word.

Whatever the charm was, it has now been completely forgotten, or at least, if anyone does remember it, it is certainly not used regularly, as it was up to 70 years ago. It has been suggested that the secret of the Word was in a particular vibration of the voice of the speaker, which for some reason the horse would always respond to.

A wealth of fascinating folklore surrounds horses and horsemanship, and many people today still firmly believe in the old superstitions. If you have a horse of your own, and even the slightest belief in charms and spells, you might like to try this old custom from Wales.

On New Year's Day wash a tea-towel, and put it out to dry on a hedge. When it is dry, rub your horse with it, and he is sure to grow healthy and strong.

CHOOSING A HORSE

Choosing a horse has always been a serious business, and not so very long ago many buyers didn't think it sufficient just to study the horse's physical condition. The superstitious among them would always look at the colour of the horse's feet.

In many areas a horse with three or four white stockings was thought to be a good buy, but some people would feel happier about buying a horse with one white fore foot and one white hind foot. In parts of Devon it was thought that just one white foot was the sign of the ideal horse.

Some of the most handsome horses in England can be seen in towns and cities – in the form of famous statues. There's something about the graceful lines and stance of a fine horse that seems to bring out the best in sculptors. Here are some well-known equestrian statues you may have seen.

GEORGE III

This imposing statue of George III mounted on a fine horse stands in the grounds of Windsor Castle, and is known to everyone as the *Copper Horse.* It is over thirty feet tall, and was made between 1824 and 1830 by Sir Richard Westmacott, who had been commissioned to make it by George IV.

George III was very fond of Windsor and he enjoyed visiting the estate farms and chatting to the locals, who soon came to call him 'Farmer George'. He even wrote agricultural papers under the pen name of Ralph Robinson. Knowing his interests, it seems strange that his son chose to have his father sculpted as a Roman emperor!

When the statue was being set up in 1830 one of the legs broke off, and a foundry was set up in the Royal park so that it could be repaired on the spot. It is said that twelve workmen sat *inside* the unfinished statue to eat their lunch!

JOHN WESLEY

This lovely equestrian statue was erected to the memory of the founder of Methodism, John Wesley. The sculptor, A G Walker, has shown him in a familiar scene, mounted on a fine horse with his Bible in his hand, dressed for the 2,500 miles he is said to have ridden in his preaching life.

The statue stands in Bristol, where Wesley founded the New Room, the oldest Methodist chapel in Britain. In his preaching days his horse was always kept at readiness near the chapel, and the stables he used are still preserved today.

LADY GODIVA

This bronze statue of the famous Lady Godiva was sculpted by Sir William Reed Dick, and was unveiled for the first time in 1949.

It was erected by the people of Coventry in memory of perhaps their most famous former inhabitant. Lady Godiva lived in the England of the AD 1000s, and was the wife of the Lord of Coventry, Leofric. According to legend, she asked her husband to reduce the heavy taxes he imposed on the people of Coventry and he agreed to do this if she rode through the town naked. She agreed and, after asking all the townspeople to stay indoors, she rode through the town on a fine horse, covered only by her long, flowing hair. Her forfeit completed, Leofric then reduced the taxes.

20

Horseback

WILLIAM III

This statue of William III stands in Bristol, and is a handsome bronze sculpture thought by many to be the finest horse statue in Britain. It is the work of John Michael Rysbrack, the Georgian sculptor who dominated this period. He was born in Antwerp, the son of a painter, but soon established himself in Britain as a great sculptor. There is a great similarity between this statue of William III and another one in Petersfield, Hampshire. In both he is depicted in Roman dress, and, although the sculptor of the second statue is not known, it seems likely that it was sculpted by Rysbrack, too.

BOADICEA

In London, at the corner of Westminster Bridge, stands an imposing group statue of the ancient tribal queen Boadicea in her chariot pulled by two rearing horses. She was a very warlike queen, and before she died in AD 62 she took part in many fierce battles, going to war in her chariot pulled by a pair of fine horses like the ones sculpted here by Thomas Thornycroft. There is only one thing missing – the horses have no reins!

CHARLES I

Another fine equestrian statue to be found in London is this one of Charles I by the Huguenot sculptor, Hubert Le Sueur. It was cast as long ago as 1633 and has an interesting history. During the Commonwealth founded by Cromwell it was removed and sold to a brazier to be melted down and, although he sold knives and souvenirs supposedly made from the metal, in actual fact he hid the statue in his garden, producing it triumphantly after the Restoration in 1660.

During the Second World War the statue was moved to Buckinghamshire for safety, and when it was erected again after the war the king had a new sword in his hand. What happened to the original? In 1867 a newspaper reporter is said to have climbed the statue to get a good view of a passing procession, clutching the sword to steady himself. The sword broke, fell among the crowds, and was never seen again, hence the need for a new one.

Another interesting fact about this statue is that, although Charles was only 5 feet 4 inches tall he evidently wanted to be taller, for he gave instructions that the statue should show him a full 6 feet tall – and that is exactly how it was made!

RECORD-BREAKING HORSES

Here are some famous and impressive horses who hold some equally famous records:

The tallest horse ever recorded was 'Firpon', a Percheron-Shire cross who stood 21.1 hands (7 feet 1 inch) tall! He weighed in at a colossal 2,976 lbs!

But that wasn't enough to beat 'Dr. Le Gear', an American Percheron who weighed 2,995 lbs! He measured 16 feet from nose to tail and died in 1919, at the age of 17.

But the heavyweight of them all was a pure-bred Belgian stallion called 'Brooklyn Supreme'. Foaled in 1928, he weighed a colossal 3,181 lbs, or 1.42 tons, shortly before his death in 1948.

Many horses have been said to reach the grand old age of 50, but the authentic old-timer of them all was 'Monty', a light draught horse who was foaled in New South Wales, Australia, in 1917 and died 52 years later in 1970.

The honour of having the longest mane on record goes to an American horse called Maud. When her mane was measured in 1905 it was found to be no less than 18 feet long!

And what about high jumpers? The official *Fédération Equestrean Internationale* high jump record was set by Captain Alberto Larraguibel Morales at Santiago, Chile, on 5th February 1949. He and his horse *Huasó* jumped the incredible height of 8 feet 1¼ inches to establish the record.

But there are other high jumpers, too. 'Golden Meade', ridden by Jack Martin cleared an unofficial 8 feet 6 inches in 1946, and in Australia 'Ben Bolt' was credited with clearing 9 feet 6 inches in 1938!

And another record set by two sturdy horses was the long trek undertaken by riders Jack Bailey and Graham Miles and their mounts 'Jason' and 'Minstrel'. Between 26th August and 5th October 1972, they trekked the 900 miles from Land's End to John O'Groats!

JOHN O'GROATS

LAND'S END

"I heard some very interesting news in the village this morning," Amy said, as she ladled out the soup at lunchtime. "There's a horse thief about! But that's not all, this one's a ghost into the bargain!"

"A ghost!" Jenny, Kevin and Ned chorused.

"Huh!" I'd just like to see a ghost steal Beauty, that's all!" Jenny said indignantly.

Doctor Gordon waited until the laughter at Jenny's remark had died down, then he spoke. "I heard a similar tale from P.C. Dickins this morning," he said, frowning slightly. "He's taking a very serious view of the matter. The thief's had seven horses already and in a lot of those cases the owners just stood by and watched because they were too scared to tackle a ghost. . . . Anyway, I think we ought to take extra care in shutting in Beauty, just in case, and I'll leave a lamp in the yard. Perhaps the light will keep the *ghost* away."

That night and every night for the rest of the week, the Gordon household kept a watchful eye on their treasured horse, but it seemed to be a waste of time. The 'ghost' seemed to have disappeared and the villagers once more began to rest easy in their beds, sure that their horses were safe in the stables.

INTO THE NIGHT

Then, just as all thoughts of ghosts had faded from their minds, the ghost thief struck again!

Jenny stirred in her sleep, disturbed by the sound of something outside. "Beauty!" She was awake in an instant at the sound of Black Beauty neighing in the stables.

Pulling on her wrap, she ran downstairs, not bothering in her haste to call anyone else. After struggling with the bolts on the front door she at last managed to open it and, seconds later, she was rushing towards the stables, where she could still hear Beauty whinnying.

The door to the stables was wide open and without hesitating Jenny ran in. At first she

couldn't see anything, but then, as her eyes grew accustomed to the light, she could see Black Beauty rearing up in his stall, neighing wildly and beside the horse . . . a terrible apparition. It was white from head to foot, and with a dreadful contorted expression on its face.

Jenny screamed out in terror and the next thing she knew the creature was brushing past her and running across the yard to a waiting horse.

The others appeared just in time to see the intruder disappear into the night.

Early the next morning P.C. Dickins arrived from the village, having met Doctor Gordon on his rounds and heard about the 'ghost' at York Cottage.

Jenny related the previous night's events as fully as she could remember them, but when she'd finished, P.C. Dickins simply sighed.

"It's always the same tale. Your description is excellent, Jenny, it fits in exactly with everyone else's tale, but that's not been much help so far. And now I've got the Squire breathing down my neck, he had two horses stolen from his stables last night. You were lucky that Beauty kicked up all that fuss."

After P.C. Dickins had gone, Kevin sat in the corner looking very thoughtful, not something that could go unnoticed for long.

"What is it?" Jenny asked. "Have you thought of something that we forgot to tell P.C. Dickins?"

"Sort of," Kevin replied, "I was just thinking back. I only saw the back of the 'ghost', as he rode off, but something struck me as being a bit strange, and I've just remembered it. Whoever it was didn't ride off into open country or towards the woods, as you would have expected. He rode off in the direction of Lawton village and that's only three miles away."

Jenny looked dubious. "Yes, but he could have been laying a false trail, or he might even have panicked and just ridden off in the first direction that came to him."

But Kevin wasn't going to be dissuaded that easily. "No!" he said, shaking his head firmly. "He turned especially to go in the direction of Lawton, that I'm sure of!"

"Perhaps we should go after P.C. Dickins and tell him then," Jenny said, after a moment's pause.

"No, I've got a better idea. Let's take Black Beauty and take a good look round before we tell anyone. I might have been mistaken. But we might even trap the 'ghost' ourselves. Imagine that!" Kevin rose to his feet. "Come on!"

Jenny looked very doubtful, but finally she shrugged her shoulders. "Oh well," she said, as she followed Kevin out, "it can't do any harm, I don't suppose."

Having told Amy that they wouldn't be gone long and that they'd be back in time for lunch, they set off for Lawton.

It didn't take very long to get there, but it did seem to be a wasted journey. Lawton was just a village like any other village, there certainly didn't seem to be anything mysterious going on.

"Oh well," Kevin said at last, flopping down on the village green to rest his aching feet, "I must have been mistaken. Apart from anything else, where would anyone hide so many horses?"

Jenny shook her head. "I don't know. Come on, we'd better be getting home. It's steak and kidney pie for lunch," she added, trying to cheer her brother up a little.

They decided to return to York cottage another way round, passing by the ruins of the old abbey.

"H'mmm," Jenny muttered, "it looks alright in the daylight, but I shouldn't like to have to pass close by late at night."

"Huh!" her brother scoffed. "It's only a heap of old stones. There's hardly anything standing, apart from that bit on the far end by the trees. Come on, let's just go and have a quick look!"

Reluctantly Jenny followed, leading Black Beauty by his reins. "We can't stay long," she said, biting her bottom lip nervously, "or we'll be late back and Amy won't be at all pleased."

But Kevin was well out of earshot already, having rushed on ahead to climb onto one of the crumbling walls. "You can see for miles from up here," he called.

But Jenny was much too concerned about Black Beauty to take any notice of Kevin.

The horse had become more and more restless as they'd drawn nearer the abbey, neighing and pawing at the ground.

"What's the matter, Beauty? Do *you* think the old abbey's a bit scarey too?" Jenny asked, stroking Beauty's nose to calm him down a little.

When Jenny looked up from calming Beauty, Kevin had disappeared. "Kevin! Kevin!" she called. "Where are you?" She was very relieved when she heard her brother's muffled voice in reply.

"I'm over here," he called. "Come and see what I've found."

Jenny made her way over in the direction of her brother's voice, still leading Beauty, who was becoming more and more restless.

Kevin sounded very excited, and so was Jenny when she saw what he'd found. Hoofprints . . . lots of hoofprints!

Cautiously they began to look round. "It's a perfect hiding place," Kevin said enthusiastically. "Why hasn't anyone thought of it before?"

"Come on, Kevin," Jenny replied nervously, "I don't like it here. Let's go and tell Father or P.C. Dickins. Beauty doesn't like it either."

"Yes, I know what you mean, it *is* a bit spooky. Come on, we'll go and tell P.C. Dickins right away." Kevin turned to leave, but it was too late. . . .

From out of the shadows leapt a frightening figure, clothed from head to toe in white. Unknown to Jenny and Kevin, they'd been watched from when they first turned towards the abbey.

You're not going anywhere!" the creature intoned in a ghostly voice. "I'm not having *my*

plans ruined by a couple of children! Why couldn't you just mind your own business, or even wait until tomorrow? I'd have been long gone by tomorrow. . . ."

"You can't keep us here!" Kevin said, sounding a lot braver than he felt. "People will come searching for us the minute they find out we're missing."

"Let them search, they won't find anything. You'll be well hidden by then."

Jenny and Kevin were tied together; it all looked hopeless. But the 'ghost' hadn't reckoned on Black Beauty. When he tried to lead the horse to where he'd kept the others hidden, Beauty reared up on his hind legs, kicking wildly at his would-be stealer.

"Good for you, Beauty! Go on, boy!" Kevin cried encouragingly. "Don't let him get you."

But Beauty wasn't only determined that his attacker wouldn't get him, he was determined to save the children too. As the 'ghost' lay stunned on the ground, Beauty galloped off in the direction of home.

"Fetch Father! Fetch Father, Beauty!" Jenny cried as the horse soared over the crumbling abbey walls and disappeared in the distance.

"You've got some hopes!" the 'ghost' said hoarsely, as he bundled Jenny and Kevin into the dank evil-smelling part of the abbey which was still standing and where he'd hidden his stolen horses. "That's only a horse, not a human being, luckily for me!"

Doctor Gordon had only just arrived back off his morning rounds. "That smells good, Amy, if it's ready we'll eat just as soon as I've washed my hands. I'm starving!"

Amy sniffed disapprovingly. "We'll have to eat alone then, Doctor, Kevin and Jenny went out this morning and I haven't seen them since, and I especially told them to be back early in time for lunch."

Doctor Gordon sighed. "Well," he said, "it's

about time they learnt their lesson. Meals are eaten on time in this house. Just serve ours, Amy, if their food is spoilt, it's spoilt!"

Ten minutes later, just as Doctor Gordon was really beginning to enjoy his steak and kidney pie, Beauty thundered up to the house.

"What the . . . !" Doctor Gordon cried, rising to his feet and peering through the dining room window. "It's Beauty, but there's no sign of either Jenny or Kevin!"

"Perhaps there's been an accident," Amy looked very worried indeed.

It took no time at all for the Doctor, who'd got used to Beauty's ways, to understand that the horse wanted the Doctor to follow him. "I'll let Beauty lead me, Amy. I think perhaps you'd better go for P.C. Dickins, just in case there's any sort of trouble. . . ."

Despite Beauty's long ride earlier in the morning, and her lightning gallop back to York cottage, she went like the wind, carrying Doctor Gordon back towards the abbey.

Beauty led him straight to where Kevin and Jenny had been tied up. "Father!" Jenny cried. "We're so glad to see you."

But Beauty's anxious pawings on the ground cut any further greetings short. The horse thief coming towards the door had noticed Doctor Gordon's arrival and was now making a run for it.

But a rugby tackle from the Doctor, something that Jenny and Kevin reminded him of later with some admiration, brought the thief to his knees. He was just unmasking the 'ghost' as P.C. Dickins arrived.

But everyone agreed that all the praise should go to Black Beauty, who'd really saved the day. . . .

Nothing new about Newmarket!

Horseracing . . . you think of the Grand National, founded in 1837. Or the Derby, in 1780. But did you know a form of the sport was practised as far back as 500 BC by the Romans? This was chariot racing, introduced from Greece, which by the first two centuries AD had reached quite devastating popularity, as we know from the many coins and other monuments illustrating this recreation.

Most of these, however, show chariot, charioteer and horse thrown to the ground, and it does seem to have been a most dangerous activity. Teams representing different quarters of the cities raced against one another, distinguished by colours, and competition was fierce – to the point where sharp knives were reputedly sometimes attached to the wheels of individual chariots, with a view to eliminating rivals.

Four vehicles generally took part in each race, each drawn by two, three, or more often four horses. The driver had to be skilful as well as brave, and indeed these men were usually professionals, hired by the rich to provide public entertainment.

The chariots themselves were of Greek design, entered from the rear, with high fronts and two wheels. The charioteers drove standing and, to achieve the breakneck speeds reached, obviously the lighter the carriage, the better. They were normally made of wood, bound with bronze. The wheels were also constructed from these materials. Two of the horses were harnessed to a pole, by a yoke, the third and fourth fastened to traces, on the outside of the yoked pair.

The horses used were not more than fifteen hands, frequently less. These were carefully bred – originally from the native mares of Apulia and sires imported from North America – and they were not permitted to race until they were five years old. They were not in fact broken until they were three years old.

At one stage, there were three Circuses – the arenas in which the races were organised – in Rome, and others in cities throughout the empire. These were enormous, well-designed places with even permanent, tiered seating, made from brick and marble when the original wooden ones were repeatedly damaged by fire. No expense was spared. A charioteer could become very rich, and a successful horse have a monument raised to it because, just as today, racing was big business. The Romans had even started betting!

Ponies of Britain

British native breeds of ponies are tremendously popular all over the world. They make excellent children's mounts, sporting ponies, and sturdy working ponies. Let's take a look at the nine major breeds.

SHETLAND

The tiny Shetland is the smallest of all British native breeds, and is a great favourite with children, especially as he is extremely friendly and good-natured. The Shetland stands only 10.2 hands high at the most, and often a hand or more less, yet it is a sturdy breed and was used for many years in farm work and as a pit pony. Shetlands may be black, bay, chestnut, brown, grey or dun.

HIGHLAND

From the smallest of the ponies to the largest, the Highland, which stands from 13 to 14.2 hands high. Highland ponies are very strong, and exceptionally sure-footed, even when climbing over rocks and rough ground. They are also very hardy in bad weather, and they are still used in the Highlands of Scotland for shepherding and forestry work, as pack horses, and for trekking. Highland ponies are shades of dun, grey, black or brown, generally with zebra markings on the forelegs.

FELL

Sure-footed Fell ponies are sturdy and strong, with a thick mane and tail to protect them in rough weather. Because of their strength and hardiness, they were once used to carry lead from mines in the north of England, over the Pennines to the docks at Tyneside, often covering up to 200 miles in a week. Fell ponies are generally dark brown, black, dark bay, or occasionally dun or grey. They stand on average 13.2 hands high.

DALES

The Dales pony is a very close relation of the Fell pony. It is slightly larger, standing from 13.2 to 14.2 hands high, as a result of crossing with the cart horse. Dales ponies are predominantly black, though sometimes brown or grey. They are very strong ponies, and as working ponies they were once used extensively for carrying heavy loads.

EXMOOR

The Exmoor pony is the oldest native breed in the British Isles. It has a harsh, springy coat and is well able to stand up to the coldest weather. Exmoor ponies are brown or bay in colour, standing up to 12.3 hands high, and they are easily recognised by their oatmeal-coloured noses. They are intelligent ponies, and make excellent mounts for children.

DARTMOOR

Dartmoor ponies are another breed which make perfect mounts for children, and they are friendly, docile and reliable. They may be any colour except piebald or skewbald, but they are generally bay, black or brown. They stand up to 12.2 hands high.

CONNEMARA

The Irish pony, the Connemara, has a rather intriguing history. It is believed to be the descendant of Spanish horses which swam ashore to Ireland from wrecked ships of the Spanish Armada in 1588. The predominant colour is grey, but they may also be black, brown, bay, dun, or occasionally roan or chestnut. They stand 13 to 14.2 hands high, and make good harness ponies, capable of travelling long distances without tiring. They are also strong working ponies.

NEW FOREST

One of the best-known and best-loved of all native breeds, the New Forest is an ideal family pony, being sturdy enough to carry adults. They may be of any colour except piebald or skewbald, but are most often bays or browns. Their average height is 13.1 hands high, and they can be as much as 14.2 hands high. They are very reliable ponies, and very sure-footed.

WELSH MOUNTAIN

The four types of Welsh pony – Welsh Mountain ponies, Sections A and B, Welsh ponies, and Welsh Cobs – are very closely related, and share many characteristics. The Welsh Mountain pony is acknowledged to be the world's most beautiful pony, and it has existed since pre-recorded history. Section A ponies stand up to 12 hands high, while Section B ponies are slightly larger. They may be all colours except piebald or skewbald. The Welsh Cob pony stands at 15 hands high, and the Welsh pony, which was produced from the Welsh Mountain Pony and the Welsh Cob, stands at approximately 13.2 hands high. The Welsh Mountain Pony is a perfect pony to ride, and it is one of the most popular of all breeds.

WHAT DO YOU KNOW?

Here's a quiz to see how much you know about famous horses, real and fictional:

1. The Duke of Wellington rode this charger at the battle of Waterloo. What is his name?

2. Emperor Caligula had many horses, but this racehorse was his great favourite – he liked him so much that he appointed him a senator! Do you know the horse's name?

3. Marion Mould is a well-known name in riding, but can you remember the name of her equally famous little showjumper, now retired?

4. In mythology, Odin had a mighty grey horse that was said to have eight legs! Do you know his name?

5. This was George III's favourite horse, and when he got older he was sold and went on to perform in many stage productions. What was his name?

6. Napoleon used this light grey Arab stallion as a charger in many of his famous battles. Do you know his name?

Answers on page 60

Excitement on Market Day

One morning Kevin came downstairs to breakfast to find Jenny busily stirring a large pan of porridge, and Albert deftly setting the table.

"What are you doing here, Albert, so early in the morning, and where is Amy?" he asked in surprise.

"Sit down and eat your breakfast and don't ask too many questions," said Ned, coming in from feeding Black Beauty just at that moment. Then, laughing at Kevin's indignant face, he added quickly, "I was only teasing you, Kevin. Albert came for the Doctor because Bessie at the inn has had an accident. She fell and injured her arm badly, and as it is market day and the inn will be very busy, Doctor Gordon has suggested that Aunt Amy lend them a hand today."

"Oh, I see," said Kevin spooning thick cream over his porridge. "Did you make this, Jenny? Perhaps *we* shall need Father's services too!"

"Not on account of Jenny's porridge, you won't!" retorted James Gordon, entering the kitchen with his bag ready to set off on his rounds. "I found it as excellent as that which Amy makes . . . she has taught you well, Jenny. And Amy has left a cold lunch and she will be back in time to prepare dinner, so we shan't starve. Albert, if you eat any more of that bread and dripping, it will be coming out of your ears."

"Sorry, Doctor, but I'm a growing lad," laughed Albert, not one bit abashed by the Doctor's remarks. "By the way, there will be a bit of excitement in the market square this afternoon. A band of strolling players are going to perform a play there. I'd like to see it, Ned, wouldn't you?"

"Oh, Father, may we all go? asked Jenny, her eyes shining with excitement. "It *does* sound fun!"

"I don't see why not," replied James Gordon, with a twinkle in his eye. "In fact, I may have a look at the play myself. I promised that I would take another look at Bessie later on today. So I shall probably see you all later. Leave my lunch ready, Jenny, as I don't know exactly when I'll be back. You and the boys can go down to the market place after lunch, but this morning I would like you to do the chores as Amy isn't here. We must all help in an emergency."

"Of course, Father," agreed Jenny at once, and the boys nodded too.

Perhaps it was the thought of the strolling players, but the afternoon seemed to arrive very quickly when, chores done and a delicious lunch eaten, Jenny and her brother with Ned and Albert, arrived in the market square.

Most of the farming business had already been completed, and as they reached the villag inn the children saw several farming friends cementing a good bargain over a glass of ale on a bench outside the inn.

Jenny spotted Black Beauty tethered nearby and realised that her father was visiting the invalid at the inn.

"Has the Doctor brought Beauty to market to sell him, Jenny?" teased one of the farmers. "He's a fine horse. *I* would buy him, for one!"

"You and everyone else around here, including Squire Armstrong," laughed Jenny merrily. "Sorry, Farmer Greenfield, but Black

Beauty is certainly not for sale. We love him too much, and besides Father needs him."

"Aye, Doctor Gordon would be lost without Beauty, and *we* would be lost without the good Doctor," cried one of the men. "Cure anything, he can, to be sure. Me rheumatics have bin ever so better since I took his medicine, and my wife insisted on calling our new baby after him because he took such good care of her. And whenever my little girl's ear hurts out he comes in all weathers, ariding old Beauty there and puts them there drops in her ears which ease her pain very soon. A real good Doctor is Master Gordon."

"My, my, my ears should be burning after all that praise!" laughed James Gordon, coming out of the inn door just at that moment. "I want no thanks for doing my job." But his heart warmed as he realised how genuinely fond of him these simple country folk were. "Now when does this play start? I think that I may have time to watch a little if no one sends for me!"

"It is due to start any minute now, Doctor, the players arrived about an hour ago," said a bluff-faced farmer. "See, there they are . . . that's the main player over there, the strange-looking cove with the shawl round his neck and the funny cap on. Looks like an actor fellow, don't 'ee?"

The Doctor hid a smile, but to his surprise the man hailed him with his stick.

"Are you a Doctor sir?" he asked in a quiet cultured voice. "Three of my young players are sick, and I would deem it a great favour on your part if you would examine them for me. I think it is merely that they have over-indulged themselves at your so excellent inn this lunch time, but I should like to make sure. My little company are treated just as if they were my own family, especially the younger ones. Please will you come?"

"Surely," replied Doctor Gordon at once, and with Jenny and the boys at his heels, he made his way over to a caravan at one side of the square.

As they approached, they all heard sounds of moaning, but as James opened the flap of the caravan he smiled, for his experienced eye had diagnosed the trouble of the three unfortunate youngsters at once . . . too much food!

"I'll examine them, of course," he said to Samuel Simpkins, the strolling player. "But I think I agree with you. Some medicine and a light diet will see them as right as rain in a few days."

"Thank goodness!" cried the old man in relief. Then he gave a cry of dismay. "But they each had a small part in the play!" he murmured. "The two boys had to prevent the wicked Squire from turning their mother out of their home while the girl rode away on a horse to bring help. And that's another thing, my horse has gone lame! Oh, dear, it looks as if I shall have to cancel my play. Everyone will be disappointed, and we shall have nothing to show today for all the hard work we have put in, and our coffers are getting quite empty. Still, that's life, and there's nothing we can do about it."

35

Jenny and the boys looked hard at each other, and then Jenny gazed appealingly at her Father.

"Now, Jenny," began Doctor Gordon for he knew exactly what was in his daughter's mind, "there could be lots of lines to learn and besides, Beauty might not like it!"

"Father, you know he would love it!" cried Jenny. "As for the lines I am sure the boys can defend themselves against the Squire . . . they've done it in real life often enough. And how many times has Beauty raced to someone's rescue? Dozens of times, as you well know. And I'm sure that Mister Simpkins will let *three* boys argue with the Squire. Ned, Kevin and Albert shall have their hour of glory."

James Gordon threw up his hands in mock despair. "What am I to do with you, Jenny?" he murmured. "Very well, but don't ride too far to bring help from the Squire . . . *I* might need Beauty to ride off to one of my patients!"

"Hurray, I knew you would agree!" cried Jenny, hugging the Doctor hard. "Come along, Mister Simpkins, tell us exactly what you want us to do!"

The old man, who had been listening to the conversation in some bewilderment, suddenly realised what was happening. A broad beam spread across his face, and he hustled the four children into his caravan, calling to the other members of his cast to gather round.

James Gordon shrugged resignedly and walked to where he would get a good view of the play. He was joined a moment later by Amy, who had just slipped out to watch for a few minutes.

"I think you're in for a big surprise, Amy," he chuckled . . . and she was!

Mister Simpkins announced the name of the play in ringing tones: *'FOILED AGAIN'* and the action began.

"Why, that's Ned . . . and Kevin . . . and Albert!" gasped Amy, as she recognised the three boys. "Whatever are they doing?"

"Acting!" laughed Doctor Gordon merrily. "Just enjoy it, Amy, I'll explain everything to you later. *They* certainly seem to be enjoying themselves. I feel quite sorry for the actor fellow playing the Squire, they're berating him quite soundly."

"Well, he deserves it!" cried Amy, quite carried away with the plot of the play. "Treating those boys and their poor mother in that way. He ought to be ashamed of himself . . . looks a bit like Squire Armstrong, too!"

The same thought had occurred to the Doctor,

and he hid a smile as he saw Armstrong, looking distinctly uncomfortable, edging away as quickly as he could.

Jenny's appearance on Beauty aroused great cheers and she rode round and round the square seeking help. Beauty added a little bit extra by refusing to let the 'Squire' leave before the 'police' arrived by rearing up on his hind legs in front of the actor, who began to think seriously of leaving the profession!

However, everything ended happily, with the Squire promising to reform and leave the family in peace. And when the actors took their bow at the end of the performance it was Beauty who received the biggest applause of all!

The ways of a WHITE HORSE

White horses have always been considered special in folklore and legend. If a witch lost her broomstick on her way to a revel she sometimes changed a sleeping mortal into a white horse and rode him to the coven meeting instead. The man never knew he had been changed except that he awoke weary and sore from his sleep!

England abounds in several white horses cut in chalk cliffs of several counties. One such famous white horse is that at Uffington in Berkshire which is believed to celebrate King Alfred's great victory over the Danes in 871, and the surrounding countryside is known as the Vale of the White Horse.

After the death of the Stuart Kings – during which time the Royal Oak was a popular inn sign as it recalled the time the young Charles II hid in an oak from Cromwell's men – many of these inn signs were repainted with a White Horse, as a compliment to the new Hanoverian King George who adopted a galloping white horse as his own royal device.

An old rhyme of Devon dwells on the importance of the number of white legs a horse has:
If you have a horse with four white legs,
Keep him not a day;
If you have a horse with three white legs,
Send him far away;
If you have a horse with two white legs,
Sell him to a friend;
But if you have a horse with one white leg,
Keep him to his end.

A white horse also featured in several rather strange cures tried out by countryfolk. A hair taken from the forelock of such a horse and eaten on bread and butter was said to be a sure cure for worms, while one hair from the tail of a white steed bound round a goitre neck made the goitre disappear!

The tooth of a white horse carried in one's pocket prevented chilblains, and a similar tooth placed beneath a pillow ensured sweet dreams free from night*mares!* Even more strange was the largely-held belief that any advice on illness given by a person riding a white horse was to be believed and acted up! But I'm sure that Doctor Gordon, riding a black horse named Beauty, is a far more reliable person to ask, don't you?

BLACK AS... BEAUTY?

Black, Beauty certainly is, but do you know:

1. Where is the Black Country?
2. Why a black doll was once on display at a marine store?
3. Who or what is 'Black Rod'?
4. Pilgrims kiss the famous Black Stone in which religious city?
5. What is the 'Black Watch'?
6. Who was 'Black Nell'?
7. What is another name for the 'Black Flag'?
8. The blackberry is the fruit of which bush?
9. Who were the Blackfeet?
10. What, in the 18th century, was known as a 'Black Dog'?

Answers on page 60

BEAUTY TO THE RESCUE

"Amy, how much longer do I have to stay in bed?" asked Jenny plaintively as the housekeeper brought up her breakfast. "I really am quite well now, you know. I hate being treated like an invalid."

"Now, Jenny, that was a bad bout of influenza you had," replied Amy, placing the tray down on the bed, and shooing the boys who had been visiting Jenny out of the room to get their breakfast downstairs. "Doctor Gordon says that you may get up after lunch and even for a little walk down by the river if you wrap up warmly enough. We don't want you ill again so soon. We really were all rather worried."

"Yes, we were, Jenny." added Kevin as he and Ned made for the door. "We hate it when you're ill . . . even if you are a bit bossy when you're well," he added with a grin.

Jenny grimaced at them and threw a pillow in their direction, narrowly missing upsetting the breakfast tray.

"Aye, I can see you are *much* better," said Amy drily, as she turned to leave. "Now, let me see clean plates when I return, Jenny, and I will tell the Doctor that your appetite's returned, and that you are well on the way to recovery."

"Amy dear, I will eat every morsel," Jenny assured her, eyeing the porridge and boiled eggs

41

with genuine relish. "Please ask Father to come and see me as soon as he has finished his breakfast. I can't lie here forever. I shall start getting fat!"

Amy laughed and went downstairs to deliver Jenny's message. Ned and Kevin were huddled in a corner, whispering and laughing together, and Amy and James Gordon exchanged resigned looks. Obviously something was brewing . . . and they hoped it was not too mischievous!

However, Doctor Gordon went up to see Jenny and, noting her empty plates and glowing cheeks, agreed that she might get up after lunch. "But don't go too far and try not to do anything too exciting. This influenza has left you weaker than you realise, Jenny," he warned his daughter.

"I promise to take care," Jenny replied sensibly. "May I get dressed and come downstairs now? I'll dress warmly, I promise."

"Very well," said James. "Great heavens, surely that isn't Beauty here in the house? Whatever are those boys thinking about?"

"Is it really Beauty?" cried Jenny jumping out of bed. "Oh, Father, I *have* missed him."

"Well, I can assure you that he is well and happy," retorted the doctor. "And put a shawl on, Miss, before you come downstairs. The morning air is still chilly."

As Jenny dressed hurriedly, she heard voices raised in protest and smothered laughter. When she got downstairs there was Beauty, standing by the sittingroom door.

"Beauty, my love, how I've missed you," cried Jenny hugging him hard, and Beauty nuzzled Jenny's hand, obviously as pleased to see her as she was to see her pet.

"*Now* will you get this animal out of my sittingroom!" ordered Amy sternly. "Doctor, have you ever seen such a thing in your life?"

"I'm prepared to see anything or anyone when these boys are around," retorted James rather grimly. "Now make yourselves scarce, boys, for the rest of the day. Amy has packed you a picnic lunch and she doesn't want to see you again until this evening. Off you go and let Amy have a little peace."

"We're going fishing," laughed Ned, as he picked up the heavy hamper. "If you're lucky, there will be fish for supper."

"I won't count on it," his aunt replied drily. "Will you be in to lunch, Doctor?"

"No, the Squire has asked me over to meet his young nephew who thinks he might like to *dabble* in medicine," James replied. "Dabble indeed! A fine doctor he will make! Not like young Doctor Martin, who is taking over my patients today so that I may have a free day for once. The Squire is sending over his carriage, so Beauty can have a rest too. I think I hear the carriage now, so I'll be off. Take care, Jenny!"

Assuring her Father that she would, Jenny helped Amy to clear the table and then she sat with a book until lunch was ready.

The sun was quite warm when Jenny set off in the early afternoon for her walk. She took the path down to the river, and sat beneath a shady tree thinking how pleasant everything was.

But suddenly the sound of voices and approaching footsteps made her start. Through a clearing she saw Jem Mason and his brother Tom and three or four more men who worked in the factory at the edge of the Squire's estate walking in the direction of the factory, carrying heavy iron bars and with grim, determined expressions on their faces.

"If we let Squire's friend install them new looms which do work o' three men, we'll all be out of jobs. Then where will 't money come from ter feed our wives and bairns?" cried Jem. "Let's smash em up, I say."

"Aye, yer right, Jem, smash the looms and save our bread!" cried Tom Mason angrily. "Nobody will stop us if they see these, and if they do, so much the worse for them!" And he waved his iron bar menacingly.

Jenny watched in dismay as the men disappeared from view. "I must tell Father!" she cried. "He will reason with them and tell them that the looms will mean more, not less work."

She rose to her feet and started back home, but she was still a few yards from Beauty's field when she felt that she could not walk another step. "I'm weaker than I thought," she murmured. "But I must get to Father and the Squire."

Beauty was contentedly munching grass in a corner of his field, but the moment he heard Jenny's voice calling to him, he trotted over to the fence.

"Jump, Beauty, come here, boy!" Jenny called urgently . . . and Beauty did just that, clearing the fence with ease and galloping quickly to Jenny's side.

"There's no time for a saddle or bridle!" Jenny murmured, as she clambered onto Beauty's back. "This is the time I find out if I could join a circus as a bareback rider!"

Jenny clung to Beauty as they cleared fields and ditches, and although at times she felt quite faint she hung on grimly.

Just when she was certain that she would have to let go, she saw her Father and Squire Armstrong obviously arguing about something.

"Father," she cried, "Jem and some men plan to smash up the looms. Can you stop them?"

"I can try," replied her Father, helping Jenny down from Beauty. "I warned you and Jackson

that this would happen if you did not explain everything properly to the men!" he said grimly to the Squire. "Pray heaven that not too much harm has been done already. Saddle up and follow me, Armstrong, as quickly as you can. I will try and talk to them. Perhaps the men will listen to me."

"Tell them . . . " began the Squire.

But James Gordon had already leaped upon Beauty's back and he was riding like the wind to the factory site.

Jackson, the owner of the factory, was at the door, surrounded by Jem and a group of men who were threatening him with their weapons, demanding that he let them in.

"Jem . . . Tom . . . men . . . listen to me!" ordered Doctor Gordon, riding up on Beauty. "Those looms mean more not less work. One man can now handle the work of three, it is true, but there are enough machines for each man already working, and the more work turned out the better the sales of cloth and better your wages. That's true, isn't it, Mr. Jackson?"

The factory owner, glad of a champion, nodded eagerly, and Jem and his mates looked at each other uncertainly.

Then Jem cried: "Well, we know that we can

trust the Doctor's word, so we'll give the looms a try, eh, men?"

The men looked uncertainly at each other, and then they all nodded reluctantly.

Mr. Jackson and James Gordon looked at each other and silently sighed with relief. A moment later up rode the Squire on a chestnut mare, followed by a groom with a pony and trap in which sat Jenny, a little paler than usual but determined not to miss any excitement.

"All's well, thanks to Jenny and Beauty," the Doctor announced quickly to Squire Armstrong. "But I do wish that people like you and Jackson would remember that your workers are human beings and deserve to be told anything which affects their lives."

The two men looked very discomforted, and Jackson muttered a gruff apology.

"Now, Jenny, if the Squire will allow it, I think is is time you were driven home," her Father said. "You've had quite enough excitement for one day."

"Very well, Father," said Jenny demurely. "But it is better than going fishing, isn't it?" And she laughed softly to herself as she imagined the boys' faces when she told them how she had spent the day.

HORSE TALES!

Almost everyone knows it is supposed to be lucky to find a horseshoe, but many other superstitions exist around the animal itself.

For example, on the day of their wedding, it is considered very good luck for the bride or groom to see a grey horse on the way to church.

In the days before the advent of the motor car, bridal carriages were always drawn by grey horses if these could be found, for apparently this similarly would contribute towards a happy life – so long as, when the bride had been set down at the church, the coachman moved some distance away before turning. To turn a horse immediately outside a church door brought terrible ill-fortune on the married couple.

Sometimes a dead gypsy's horses have been slaughtered with him. Like the peoples of the Middle East who in the past buried goods and animals with their dead master, this has on occasions been deemed necessary to establish good relations for the person in his after-life.

An old Yorkshire superstition says that, if you see a white horse on leaving home that's unlucky. This is certainly confirmed if you go on to meet a field of horses, all standing with their backs to the hedge – for that means a storm's on the way!

All Kinds of Horses

1. What sign does every donkey have on its back?

2. By what other name is a Horse-gowan better known?

3. What famous holiday resort is well-known for its horse trams?

4. Who, according to mythology, created the first horse?

5. What is an 'iron horse'?

6. Rosabelle was the favourite palfrey of which famous Queen?

7. In which well-known book do Dick Turpin and Black Bess appear?

8. Bucephalus was the charger of Alexander the Great. What does this horse's name mean, and how did Alexander remember him when Bucephalus died?

9. What two virtues is a horse said to represent in art?

10. Which saint is said to have 'shoed the devil'?

Check your answers on page 60

HORSES IN RHYME

1. I had an ivory manger,
   And drank from a golden pail,
   I was even made a consul,
   And wore jewels in my tail.

   Who am I?

2. My master was called Crookback,
   King Richard of ill-fame,
   A colour and a county,
   Will for you complete my name.

   Who am I?

3. I'm the subject of a painting,
   I was ridden at Waterloo,
   I am a fine white stallion,
   My rider is well-known too.

   Who am I?

4. Long ago in Camelot
   I was brave King Arthur's mare,
   I was called 'the curvetter',
   And everyone at me did stare.

   Who am I?   Answers on page 60

LOST!

"Who'd have thought it! *Ha ha! Ha ha!*" Jenny burst out laughing, despite her attempts to keep a straight face.

Kevin spluttered alongside her, while Ned shifted uncomfortably in his seat, blushing crimson and looking as though he wished he was a hundred miles away.

"What's all this? Can I be let in on the joke?" Doctor Gordon looked questioningly at his children as he came into the room.

Kevin and Jenny looked at one another mischievously. "Ned's in love!" Jenny finally managed to say, choking with laughter.

Ned went redder still; a fact which didn't escape the Doctor.

"In love?" he said, raising his eyebrows in surprise and trying desperately to keep from smiling. "Well, love's a very serious thing. I don't see what there is to laugh about!"

Jenny and Kevin continued giggling.

"And . . . it's very private! So I don't think we'll discuss the matter any further. Ned, will you go and tell Amy we're about ready to eat."

Ned, glad of the escape, disappeared rapidly in the direction of the kitchen, leaving Doctor Gordon to 'shush' his children into some semblance of silence before his return.

Later that afternoon, his chores finished, Ned could be seen creeping away from York House in the direction of Mill Woods and if Kevin and Jenny had spotted him, they'd have known exactly where he was going . . .

The gipsy encampment lay just inside Mill Woods, in a large clearing by the stream that fed the wheel of the mill just beyond the woods. It seemed a perfect setting and certainly the gipsies seemed to think so, for they'd been camped in the spot all summer.

Ned made his way towards the green and yellow caravan that he'd come to know so well. For a moment he paused. "Love!" he muttered, "In love! What rubbish they talk! Anna's just a friend. And anyway, her mum makes smashing stews in that pot over the open fire; but I'd better not let Amy know!"

"Ned! Ned! I'm over here!" The sound of Anna's voice broke into Ned's thoughts and he turned to where Anna was standing and waving.

No sooner had Ned arrived by her side than Anna began talking excitedly. "We're leaving, Ned. Day after tomorrow as soon as the sun rises we'll be on our way, back on the open road again. Isn't it exciting?"

Ned nodded, trying to look pleased at Anna's news; but, try as he could, he couldn't think of anything suitable to say. But Anna didn't seem to notice.

"Can you come for a picnic tomorrow, Ned? It'll be the last chance I'll have to see you before I leave. I'll see to all the food, all you'll have to do is come. But can you borrow a horse? There's a secret place that I've found that I want

to show you before I go."

Once he was back at York House, Ned began to cheer up a little. Perhaps things wouldn't be so bad after all and at least Kevin and Jenny would have to stop making fun of him over Anna.

But a few minutes later Ned's happiness disappeared once more. . . .

"I'm sorry, Ned, but I just can't spare Beauty for a whole day, I've got my rounds to do. If it was late afternoon, fine. But as it is . . . ." Doctor Gordon looked apologetically at Ned. He knew that Ned was disappointed, but there was nothing he could do.

Ned tried to think of a way round his troubles

all day, but there didn't seem to be any solution, and he went to bed feeling very sorry for himself.

By early next morning, however, he'd come to a decision. Silently, long before the rest of the household was awake, Ned slipped out to the stables, silently he saddled up Beauty and minutes later he was riding out towards Mill Woods.

"Where's Ned this morning? He's not ill, is he?" Doctor Gordon looked at Ned's empty place.

Jenny and Kevin shrugged their shoulders in reply.

"Well, I've called him three times!" Amy replied briskly. "And I've warned that boy before. He's just lazy, that's all. He can stay in bed all day for me, but he'll get no meals."

The Doctor and his children looked at each other and then began eating their porridge. There was no arguing with Amy when she was in one of these moods.

It wasn't until everyone was having their last cup of tea that anyone spoke at all.

"Jenny," the Doctor said, breaking the long silence, "do you think you could saddle Beauty up for me this morning. I've got some papers I want to collect together, and I want to get an early start. Two pairs of hands and all that."

The Doctor was in his study when he heard Jenny's urgent shouts. "Beauty's gone! The stable's empty and his saddle and everything have disappeared."

Amy and Jenny arrived at the study door at the same time. Amy spoke quietly. "Ned's gone too. I went up to get him out of bed and he was missing!"

Doctor Gordon looked grim. "Well, I think we'll ignore the whole matter for the time being. I'm sure the mystery, if mystery it is, will be solved before nightfall. Meanwhile, I have work to do. I'll walk into the village and see if I can borrow Bill Wright's horse for my rounds."

The rest of the day passed very quietly indeed, although York House seemed to buzz with an expectant air as though waiting for something to happen.

Amy waited until the last possible moment before drawing the curtains and lighting the lamps, for they only served to draw attention to the deepening gloom both inside and outside the house.

Doctor Gordon looked up from the book he was reading and sighed. "Well, there's nothing we can do in the darkness, but first thing tomorrow morning I'll have to go into the village to see P.C. Dickins."

Amy was up especially early the next morning, partly because she couldn't sleep and partly in the hope that Ned might somehow have returned during the night without her knowing. But his bed was still made as Amy had left it, unslept in.

After setting the table for breakfast, she opened the back door and glanced across to the stables . . . but something was wrong! The door that had been locked the night before was now slightly open. Her heart thumping wildly, she crossed the yard to investigate.

Quietly she opened the door of the barn and crept in. At first she couldn't see anything in the gloom, and then in the corner she caught sight of something . . . or someone huddled in the far corner . . . . It was Ned!

"Ned! Ned! Are you alright?" Amy shook his shoulder gently.

"M'mmm? Oh, oh, Aunt Amy, it's you." Ned opened his eyes sleepily, then suddenly he stiffened with fear, his eyes clouding over. "I . . . I've lost Beauty. . . ."

"Lost? Where did you lose him?" Amy enquired worriedly.

But before Ned could reply, Doctor Gordon had arrived on the scene. A look of relief passed over his face.

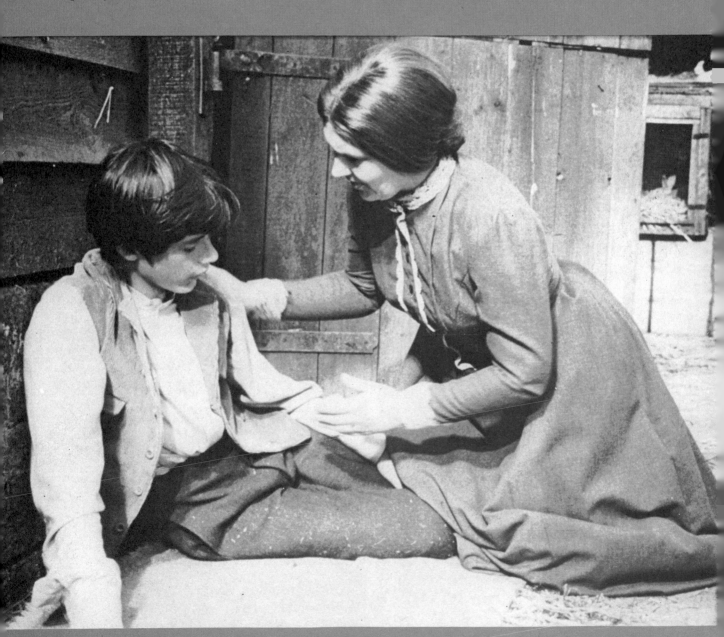

'Well, at least you've turned up. We were getting quite worried, Ned. Whatever made you stay away?"

Ned began to explain how he'd taken Beauty early the morning before, intending only to ride over and tell Anna that he couldn't go on the picnic, but how he'd been persuaded to ride out and see Anna's secret hiding place.

" . . . But when we came out of the cave Beauty had gone," Ned looked very upset. "I promise I tied him up well, Doctor Gordon, honestly. But he'd just disappeared. Well, Anna and I searched everywhere for him, but it was no good. And it was getting later and later and I was worried. I thought you might think that I'd disobeyed you on purpose. So I stayed in the woods until it was quite dark, but then I got to

thinking that I'd have to explain to you some time, so I came home. But you'd all gone to bed by that time." Ned glanced down at his grubby fingers, afraid of what the Doctor would say.

Doctor Gordon smiled kindly. "I think we'd better go in and have some breakfast, the world always looks better on a full stomach," he said. "Come on, Ned, don't look so worried. If ever there was a horse who could look after himself, that horse is Black Beauty!"

However, no one was expecting the sound of hoofs in the yard, or the sound of a familiar neighing before they'd even finished breakfast, but that was what had happened . . . .

Ned reached the nearest window first. "It's Anna!" he cried. "She's got Beauty with her!"

It was quite a crush, with five people all trying to get through one narrow doorway at once, but they eventually managed to sort themselves out, with Ned out in the lead.

Anna looked a little taken aback at the response to her arrival, but she seemed slightly reassured at the sight of Ned.

She waited until they'd all finished firing questions at her and then she started shifting uncomfortably from one foot to another as she began to speak.

"When we set off early this morning," she explained, "we took the turnpike road for the south. We hadn't gone far when we caught up with another group of our people, who were going the same way, so we joined up with them. It was only when we'd been travelling half-a-mile or so that we noticed Beauty. He'd been tied to one of the caravans. I'm afraid he's been badly whipped . . . " she added.

Jenny rushed over. "Oh, Beauty!" she cried. "What have they done to you?"

Beauty's back still showed the terrible weals left by a severe whipping. Doctor Gordon put his arms around his daughter's shoulders to comfort her.

"Don't worry, Jenny, I'm sure Beauty will be alright. He probably put up such a fight that it was the only way his thieves could control him."

Anna, who'd been standing quietly to one side beside Ned, interrupted. "I'll have to go now, if I'm to catch up with the others. Father said they'd wait at the crossroads for me. And he said not to bother any further about the thieves, we have our own Romany ways of dealing with them. I'm glad that Black Beauty is safe. He's a beautiful horse," she said wistfully.

"Well, you'll have to come and see him the next time you're over this way," Amy said kindly. "We'd *all* be pleased to see you . . . and perhaps you'd like to sample my stew . . . although I'm sure it's not as good as your mother's!" Amy stole a look at Ned, a twinkle in her eyes.

Ned blushed furiously, but the others were all too busy laughing to notice . . . .

A HORSEY CROSSWORD

Clues Across:

1. and 1 down. Dick Turpin's famous horse (5, 4)
4. Piece of equipment usually found on a rider's heels (4)
5. Lipizzaners are the famous grey horses found at the .... Riding School (7)
7. A horse with pricked ...... is a happy horse! (4)
9. .... Friesian and .... Prussian are both breeds of horses (4)
11. A lively young female horse (5)
12. Two types of horse that share the same name, the ....-Arab and the ....-Norman (5)
13. One of the most famous horse races, also a hat (5)

Clues Down:

1. See 1 across
2. Perhaps the most popular of all breeds of horses (4)
3. An eatable comb? (5)
4. Small pony native to Scotland, sometimes called a 'sheltie' (8)
6. The Salerno and the Calabrese are both bred in this country (5)
8. One of the great draught breeds, with heavy hair on the legs (5)
10. A horse's footwear? (4)

Answers on page 60

Snakes and Scarabs

One warm autumn afternoon Ned was making his way home to York House thinking happily how pleased his Aunt Amy would be with the handkerchief full of blackberries which he had just gathered from the brambles near the Squire's estate, when he was suddenly seized roughly and shook hard.

"And what have you got in that handkerchief, you young rascal?" asked a sarcastic but cultured voice. "Do you know that you are trespassing on the Squire's estate?"

Ned opened his lips to protest, but before he could speak, up rode the familiar figure of Squire Armstrong.

"You can let that boy go, Travers," he said curtly. "He is the nephew of James Gordon's housekeeper, and as such I allow him and the Gordon children to take this short cut home. Been collecting blackberries, have you, young Ned? Well, tell Amy to remember me when she makes her jam."

The Squire did not seem to notice that Ned seemed reluctant to open his handkerchief to reveal the full contents. Armstrong was too busy talking to his companion who, Ned learned from the conversation, was visiting the Hall.

"James Gordon, you say?" echoed the man in an interested tone. "The Doctor with the horse called Black Beauty? The horse you say is fit for a young rajah?"

"Indeed he is, but Gordon will never sell. Money means little to him. He is a man of simple needs, and the family love that horse far too much to ever sell him!" Armstrong retorted.

Colonel Travers laughed scornfully. "Every man has his price!" he argued confidently. "Just introduce me to Gordon and you will see."

Ned continued on his way, filled with anger at the man's words. Who was this unpleasant stranger, he wondered, who seemed so determined to buy Black Beauty.

"I'm glad I didn't show them what else I found beside the blackberries," he murmured aloud. "I'm sure that old Colonel would have claimed it . . . and I don't think that it belongs to him at all."

"What are you muttering about, Ned?" asked a laughing voice behind him, and with a start Ned looked up and saw Jenny smiling at him as she reined Beauty to a halt.

Ned quickly explained what had just happened and he untied his red handkerchief to reveal a cluster of juicy blackberries and a pendant, shaped like a beetle, gleaming silver amongst the dark berries.

"What is it?" asked Jenny curiously. "It looks as if it came from across the seas."

"Indeed, young miss, you are right. The scarab is mine and it was given to me by my young master, the rajah, in India, before I left my native shores," said a soft voice.

Turning in surprise, Jenny and Ned saw a slim, dark-skinned figure dressed in a blue robe and a yellow silk turban around his head.

"Do not fear me," he added gently. "I mean you no harm. Indeed, I come to warn you about the Colonel. He is a man without honour. He wormed his way into the rajah's service with cunning tricks. He has come to England to buy horses for my master, and I have come to try and find proof that he is a wicked man so that my master will dismiss him."

"I hope that you find it!" cried Ned eagerly, as he handed over the scarab pendant and watched Ranji put it around his neck. "But you need not worry. The Doctor will never sell Black Beauty."

"I have no fear of that, for everyone in the village has told me of your love for the horse and I know that your father is a good man. No, my young friends, what I fear is the vengeance of that wicked man when he discovers that, for once in his life, he cannot buy something with money. Be on your guard, for he will stop at nothing to gain his revenge," said Ranji.

"Oh, he cannot harm us here in England," Jenny assured him with a smile. "We have an excellent police force and Father will make sure that we come to no harm. But thank you kindly for your concern. I hope that we shall see you again before you return home. Come along, Ned, it is nearly lunch time. Amy sent me to look for you. It's apple dumplings for dinner. You don't want to miss those."

And so, waving goodbye to their new friend, the children hurried home.

"He does seem a nasty customer," said Kevin as Jenny poured out her story to him and Amy over dinner. "I think you'd better tell Father."

"If it's about Colonel Travers I have already seen the fellow, a disgrace to the good name of the Indian army," said Jenny's father as she ran out to greet him on the Doctor's return from his rounds. "I firmly refused his offer, and I have told him to steer clear of York Cottage or it will be the worst for him!"

"Good for you, Father, the man's a real villain!" cried Jenny, and she told the Doctor all about Ned's meeting with the Colonel.

Much comforted by Doctor Gordon's words, Jenny went to bed quite happily, but Ned was very uneasy in his mind. He remembered the Colonel's cruel grip on his shoulders and his cold eyes and mocking words. Colonel Travers could be a vengeful man, of that Ned felt quite sure.

So, waiting until the household was sound asleep, he crept out quietly and went to sleep in the stable, near Black Beauty's stall. "Now I can keep a really close guard on you, Beauty," he murmured as he lay down on a bed of straw, quite prepared to stay awake all night if necessary.

But, alas for Ned's good intentions, his eyes grew heavy and gradually closed until he was sound asleep.

But Ned had quick ears, even in sleep, and a sound from the doorway caused him to start up and wake. Through half-closed eyes he saw a dark figure release something from a basket which slithered down among the straw.

"Stop! What are you doing?" cried Ned in alarm, and he got up quickly and ran off after the intruder.

But the man had a horse waiting outside, and despite Ned's gallant attempts to cling to the bridle he was kicked cruelly aside and fell down, injuring his knee.

"Help! Help! Doctor Gordon! Jenny! Come

quickly!" he cried urgently, as he stumbled back in the cottage to raise the alarm.

The Doctor's strong arms caught Ned as he fell, for Jenny had awoken from an uneasy sleep and she had got up with the intention of creeping down to the stable to make sure that Beauty was safe.

She was just in time to see the stranger ride off after ill-treating Ned, and her anxious calls were quickly answered by her Father and Kevin.

"Never heed me, Doctor, 'tis Beauty who's in danger," gasped Ned. "The rogue has let loose a snake in the hay near Beauty's stall. And not a harmless snake, I'll be bound."

"It's probably that rascally Travers!" cried James Gordon, as they all hurried over to the stable. "Give Ned a warm drink, Amy, and let him rest. I will attend to him shortly."

Through the open doorway Jenny saw Beauty rearing up in a panic. His keen ears had heard the almost silent slithering of the snake as it made its way towards him. Animal instinct warned Beauty that he was in danger, and the horse was determined to avoid it at all costs.

"Oh, Father, what can we do?" gasped Jenny in dismay. "If the snake is indeed dangerous, you also run the risk of being bitten."

James Gordon paused for a moment, his thoughts racing, trying to find the best solution when, suddenly, he and Jenny heard the sound of piping music.

As they neared Beauty, they saw Ranji on the other side, with a reed basket and a pipe between his lips. Slowly the snake responded to the music,

Check your answers

WHAT DO YOU KNOW?

1. Copenhagen; 2. Incitatus; 3. Stroller; 4. Sleipnir; 5. Adonis; 6. Marengo.

BLACK AS BEAUTY

1. The Midlands. 2. To show that secondhand garments were sold there. 3. The person responsible for maintaining order in the House of Lords, and for summoning the Commons to the Lords when necessary. 4. Mecca. 5. A famous Highland regiment which wears a tartan of the same name. 6. Wild Bill Hickok's famous mare. 7. The Jolly Roger, the pirate flag. 8. The bramble. 9. A tribe of North American Indians. 10. A counterfeit silver coin actually made from pewter.

ALL KINDS OF HORSES

1. A cross. 2. An ox-eye daisy. 3. Douglas, Isle of Man. 4. Poseidon. 5. A steam train. 6. Mary, Queen o'Scots. 7. Rookwood. 8. Ox-head. When Bucephalus died, Alexander built the city of Bucephala as a memorial to him. 9. Courage and generosity. 10. St. Dunstan.

HORSES IN RHYME

1. Caligua's horse, Incitatus. 2. Richard III's horse, White Surrey. 3. Napoleon's horse, Marengo. 4. King Arthur's horse, Lamri.

A HORSEY CROSSWORD

Across:

1. Black; 4. spur; 5. Spanish; 7. ears; 9. east; 11. filly; 12. Anglo; 13. Derby.

Down:

1. Bess; 2. Arab; 3. curry; 4. Shetland; 6. Italy; 8. Shire; 10. shoe.

raising its ugly head and gazing with an unblinking stare at the Indian, who continued to play calmly.

Jenny and her Father watched the whole scene in amazement, and the music even seemed to calm Beauty, who became much less restless, as if sensing that Ranji was trying to help him.

Suddenly, while still playing, the Indian swiftly leaned forward and seized the snake behind its neck. A quick squeeze and the snake

was deposited out of harm's way in the basket.

"You were wonderful! And so brave!" cried Jenny as she hurried over to calm Beauty. "But how did you know what was happening?"

"I witnessed your Father's meeting with the Colonel," said Ranji with a grave smile. "I knew the Colonel was angry, and so I kept watch on the great house. When Colonel Travers came out I followed him. I always carry my pipe and I was glad to do so when I saw the Colonel with the snake basket. See, proud man that he is, his mark is on the basket."

"His initials, you mean," said Doctor Gordon. "Well, the rogue's certainly done for here in England, and the sworn statement which I shall make for you before a magistrate will show your young rajah what a villain he is. But you were a brave fellow with that snake, Ranji. Goodness knows what would have happened if it had bitten you. I have no snake serum."

"My scarab would have protected me," replied the Indian, fingering the silver beetle. "It protects against all poisons."

"But surely . . ." began Jenny, but a look from her Father told her to stop.

Later, after explanations had been made to Amy and Ned's injury had been seen to, Jenny said, "Surely you don't really believe in the magic of the scarab, Father?"

"I do not, but Ranji does, which is all that matters," said James Gordon. "And who are we to say it does not work? Just be thankful, Jenny, that he saved Beauty from a painful death."

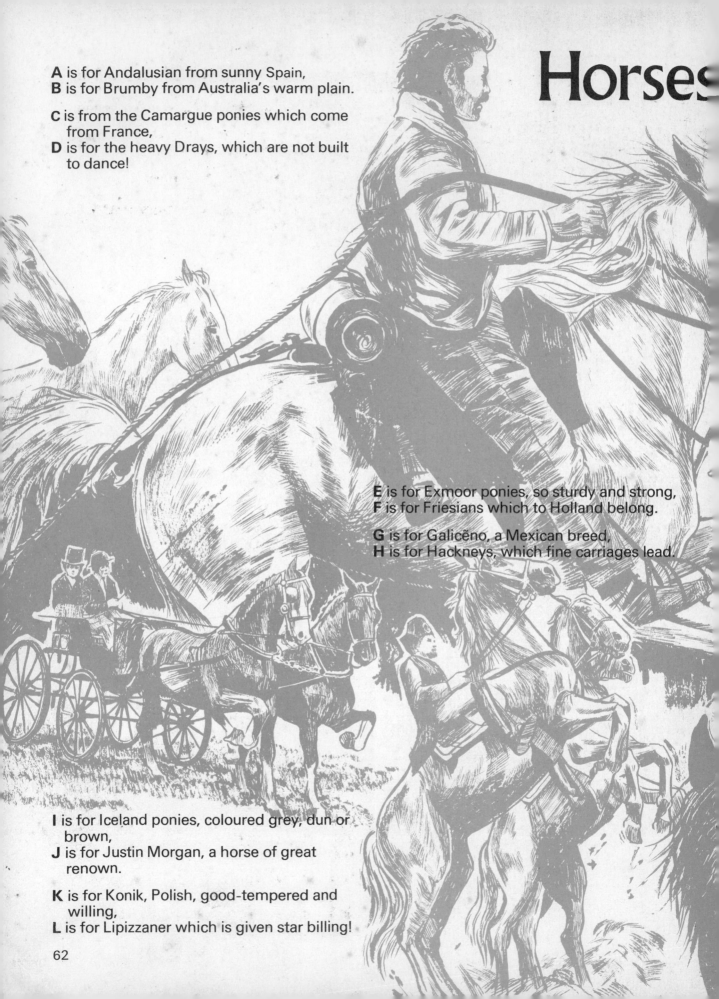

Horses

A is for Andalusian from sunny Spain,
B is for Brumby from Australia's warm plain.

C is from the Camargue ponies which come
   from France,
D is for the heavy Drays, which are not built
   to dance!

E is for Exmoor ponies, so sturdy and strong,
F is for Friesians which to Holland belong.

G is for Galicẽno, a Mexican breed,
H is for Hackneys, which fine carriages lead.

I is for Iceland ponies, coloured grey, dun or
   brown,
J is for Justin Morgan, a horse of great
   renown.

K is for Konik, Polish, good-tempered and
   willing,
L is for Lipizzaner which is given star billing!